Amazing Tricks of Real Spies

James de Winter

Capstone
press

Mankato, Minnesota

Fact Finders is published by Capstone Press,
a Capstone Publishers company.
151 Good Counsel Drive, P.O. Box 669,
Mankato, Minnesota 56002.
www.capstonepress.com

First published 2009

Library of Congress Cataloging-in-Publication Data

De Winter, James.
  Amazing Tricks of Real Spies / by James de Winter.
  p. cm. -- (Fact finders. Extreme explorations!)
  Includes bibliographical references and index.
  Summary: "Explores the techniques and tools used by
spies"--Provided by publisher.
  ISBN 978-1-4296-4563-8 (library binding)
  ISBN 978-1-4296-4612-3 (pbk.)
1. Spies--Juvenile literature. 2. Espionage--Juvenile
literature. I. Title. II. Series.

UB270.5.D44 2010
327.12--dc22

2009027853

Produced for A & C Black by
MONKEY PUZZLE MEDIA LTD
Monkey Puzzle Media Ltd
48 York Avenue
Hove BN3 1PJ, UK

Editor: Susie Brooks
Design: Mayer Media Ltd
Picture research: Lynda Lines
Series consultants: Jane Turner and James de Winter

This book is produced using paper that is made from
wood grown in managed, sustainable forests. It is natural,
renewable, and recyclable. The logging and manufacturing
processes conform to the environmental regulations of the
country of origin.

Printed in Malaysia by Tien Wah Press (Pte.) Ltd

102009
005558

Picture acknowledgements
Alamy pp. 13 (Utah Images/NASA), 14 (Photo12), 24
(Photo12); Beijing Military Museum p. 29 top right; Corbis
pp. 4 (Bettmann), 26 (Anna Clopet), 27 (Image Source);
Crown Copyright p. 25 all; Getty Images pp. 1, 5, 9 (Ted
Kinsman), 10 left, 15, 17, 21 both (AFP); International Spy
Museum pp. 7, 22 left, 29 bottom; Kobal Collection pp. 18
(Cinema Center), 28 (Danjaq/EON/UA); MPM Images
pp. 20, 23 both; PA Photos pp. 8 (Matt Cilley/AP), 19
(David Furst/AP); Photoshot p. 6 (UPPA); Thomas
Jefferson Foundation p. 22 right; Touchstone Pictures
pp. 10–11 (Buena Vista Pictures); U.S. Department of
Defense p. 12; U.S. Navy p. 16.

The front cover shows a spy's eye peeping through a
keyhole (iStockphoto).

Every effort has been made to contact copyright holders
of material reproduced in this book. Any omissions will
be rectified in subsequent printings if notice is given to the
publishers.

CONTENTS

Abbreviation km stands for kilometers

Being James Bond

What's it like to be James Bond? You get gadgets, a cool car, and fame! There are spies like Bond in real life too—but they don't go around being quite so flashy.

Klaus Fuchs, a Russian spy, was imprisoned for stealing weapon secrets during World War II.

For your eyes only

In the 16th century, a spy working for Queen Elizabeth I marked his secret messages with **00**—a code meaning "for your eyes only." That gave James Bond's creator the idea for 007!

James Bond may be famous, but real spies try hard to stay unknown. Their job is to find out other people's secrets, whether they are war plans, weapons, or just clever ways of making lots of money.

silencer a device that absorbs the sound from a gun, making it much quieter

Spy guns can be fitted with **silencers**, so no one will hear the bang.

It might look normal, but this jacket could be bullet-proof or contain a hidden camera.

Spying can be dangerous—especially if you're caught. So spies need skill and science on their side. They use the latest technology to help them gather **intelligence** without ending up in prison, or worse.

James Bond is the spy who will never die—only because he's made up!

intelligence secret information, especially from governments and armies

Stop bugging me!

Barging up to the enemy with a film crew would not do a spy any favors. But spies can still record what they shouldn't, using tiny hidden cameras and bugs.

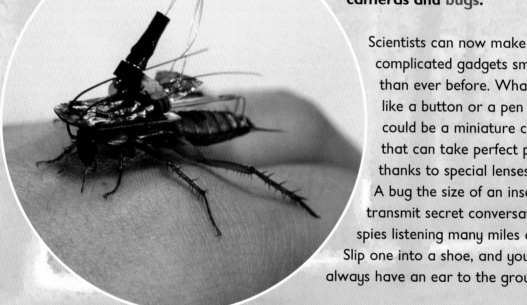

This live cockroach is carrying a mini-camera on its back! It can creep under doors to help spies see what's going on.

Scientists can now make complicated gadgets smaller than ever before. What looks like a button or a pen cap could be a miniature camera that can take perfect pictures thanks to special lenses inside. A bug the size of an insect can transmit secret conversations to spies listening many miles away. Slip one into a shoe, and you'll always have an ear to the ground . . .

Fly on the wall

The U.S. military is working on designs for tiny flying robots that look like insects but have spy bugs and cameras on board.

bug a device that records and transmits (sends) sounds to special receivers

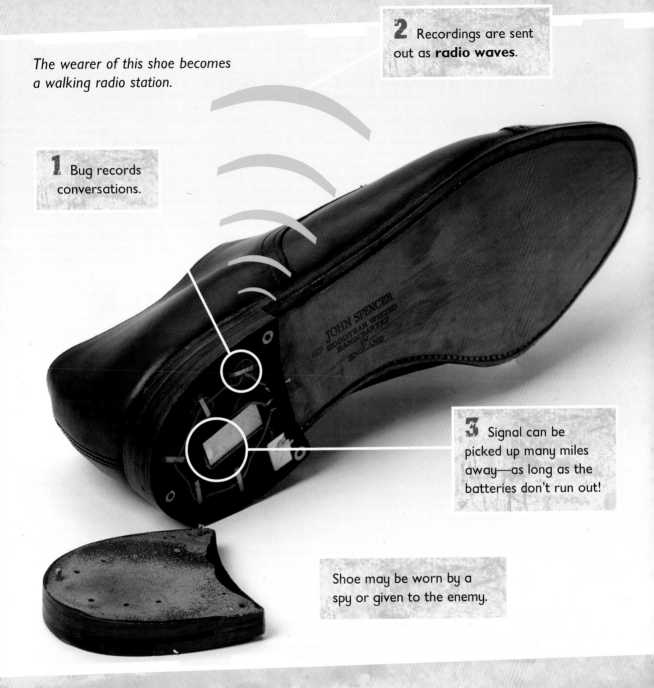

The werer of this shoe becomes a walking radio station.

2 Recordings are sent out as **radio waves**.

1 Bug records conversations.

JOHN SPENCER
GOODYEAR WELTED
HANDCRAFTED
IN
ENGLAND

3 Signal can be picked up many miles away—as long as the batteries don't run out!

Shoe may be worn by a spy or given to the enemy.

radio waves waves of energy that travel silently and invisibly through the air

Eyes in the dark

Under cover of darkness, you can get away with anything—can't you? Think again. Spies have ways of seeing in the dark—and so do their enemies.

Night vision goggles allow you to see without being seen.

Keeping track

Thermal imaging can see where people have been, even if they're not there anymore! It can tell where ground has been walked on, driven on, or dug up to bury something.

Our eyes need light to be able to see. But with night vision equipment, a spy can snoop for secrets in a pitch-black room. Some **night vision** gadgets collect tiny amounts of light that we don't notice. Others use thermal imaging to detect warm things like people . . . including spies escaping on the run.

thermal imaging making pictures using infrared heat energy instead of light

A thermal imaging camera catches people walking in the woods.

People give off heat, even when standing still.

Don't run—you'll just get hotter, brighter and easier to spot!

Trees and ground show up a different color because they are cool.

night vision ability to see in the dark using infrared heat energy

I see-see TV you!

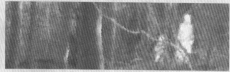

A safe way of spying is to do the job from a distance. With **CCTV**, spies can stay hidden—and have eyes in hundreds of places at once.

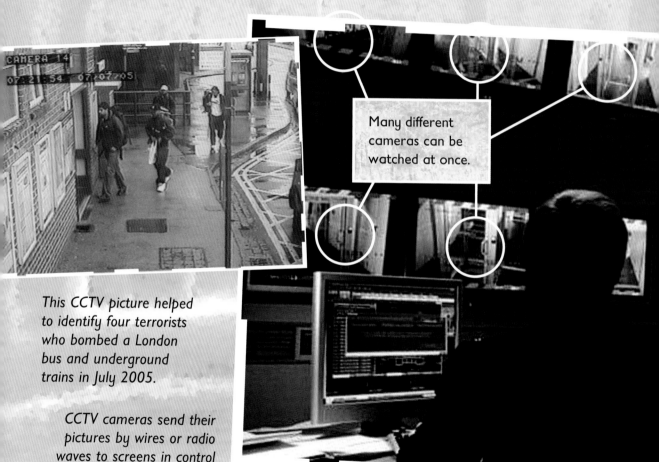

Many different cameras can be watched at once.

This CCTV picture helped to identify four terrorists who bombed a London bus and underground trains in July 2005.

CCTV cameras send their pictures by wires or radio waves to screens in control rooms like this.

CCTV (closed-circuit TV) a way of filming streets, shops, and other places

CCTV cameras lurk in all sorts of places, filming all day, every day. They may spot a suspect wandering home, or catch a criminal in action. The pictures are transmitted to nearby TV screens and saved onto giant computers. This helps spies, police, and governments track down trouble, without having to budge from their seats.

Always watching

There are now millions of CCTV cameras. Some of us may be filmed over 300 times a day. Make sure you behave yourself!

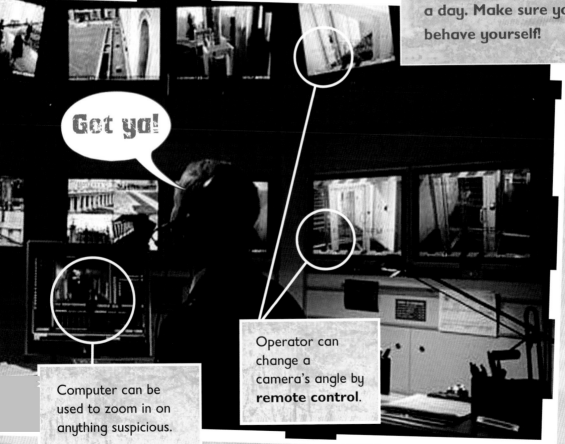

Got ya!

Computer can be used to zoom in on anything suspicious.

Operator can change a camera's angle by **remote control**.

remote control operating a device from a distance, often using radio signals

High spy!

Imagine terrorists were planning to attack your country. How would you find their base? You'd get a pretty good view from the sky and an even better one from space.

Satellite photos can show a vehicle but not its license plate.

Spy **satellites** act like massive digital cameras, traveling around Earth in space. They take pictures of the ground below them as they pass over, using gigantic lenses to zoom close-in. Information about how they work is mostly top secret, but we know that they beam radio signals back to Earth. These are captured by spy computers, which display the photos on screen.

A satellite photograph reveals a terrorist training camp in Afghanistan.

Flying photos

Early spy satellites delivered their pictures by dropping camera film attached to parachutes. Military planes would catch them in midair!

satellite a machine that is sent into space to collect and send back information

Satellites fly 100–1,240 miles (160–2,000 km) above Earth.

Gravity and high speed keep the satellite moving in a circular path.

Radio signals beam pictures back to Earth.

gravity a pulling force between all objects in the universe

Snooperscopes

You're under the sea in a secret submarine, spying on enemy ships. No one can see you deep down there—but you can see them, thanks to a periscope.

Sean Connery looks into a submarine periscope in the film The Hunt for Red October.

Periscopes allow spies to see around corners, over walls—and up through the ocean. They work by using mirrors or **prisms** to bounce light from one place to another. A mirror at the top of the periscope **reflects** light down into a second mirror at the bottom. The light is then reflected toward the viewer's eye.

The most advanced periscopes have lenses in the middle of the tube. These enlarge the view you see, so the periscope acts as a telescope, too!

Sneaky specs

Have you ever wished you had eyes in the back of your head? Some spies wear sunglasses with mirrors on the inside, so they can see what's going on behind them!

prism a triangular block of glass or plastic that can bend the path of light

Mirrors inside the tube reflect light down to the bottom.

Mirrors must be set at exactly the right angle.

You're being watched if you're over here!

Light travels down through the periscope.

Light reflects off of bottom mirror and travels toward the eye.

A Kosovan soldier keeps an eye on the enemy using a homemade periscope.

reflect to bounce back rays of light

Invisible ears

Spies might check their rooms for bugs and make their phone calls in private—but that doesn't mean no one hears what they say.

*Inside this **radome**, anyone's mobile phone conversation could be recorded—even yours.*

Every phone call, fax and e-mail that's ever sent is transmitted along wires or as radio waves though the air. **Intelligence networks** have special equipment that can intercept these messages and find out what anyone is saying. If spies want to know what foreign spies are up to, they can search for certain keywords. Computers will pick these words out of all the babble, saving a lot of listening time!

radome a weatherproof dome covering radio receivers

Hidden receivers capture radio, phone, fax, and e-mail conversations.

Onboard computers work out which messages matter.

Jibber jabber

Global ears

ECHELON is a secret spy system that governments use to tap into communications around the world. It recognizes words in every single language!

This U.S. spy plane is like a vacuum cleaner in the sky, sucking up everyone's words!

intelligence networks groups of spies working for governments or businesses

Masters of disguise

If you ever met a spy, you probably wouldn't know it. In fact, the American woman you're talking to might actually be a Russian man! Spies need to blend in with whoever they're watching—which is why they are masters of disguise.

Today's spies have impressive wigs, makeup and even **voice changers** to help them create a **cover**. They may spend years and years pretending to be someone else—but, these days, that's not as easy as it sounds.

Computers can now recognize your walk, sniffer dogs can tell your smell . . . and even if you manage to change these things, your eyeballs will give you away.

With modern makeup, you really can get into someone else's skin! Is he who he says he is?

voice changer   a device that changes the sound of your voice

A man has his iris scanned at a security check.

Machine scans the eyeball.

Everyone's iris is unique.

Details about the person are kept on file.

Scanner works even through contact lenses.

SecuriMetrics   PIER 2·3

Eye spy

The colored part of your eye, called the iris, has a pattern unlike anyone else's. Just like fingerprints, it can be scanned and used to prove who you are!

cover a false identity

19

Dead-letter box

A dead-letter box sounds like something used by a corpse—but in fact it's a place where spies leave secret messages! Spies do this when it's too dangerous for them to meet.

Messages need to be hidden where they won't **rot**, blow away or get eaten by a curious animal. One trick is to bury them underground inside sealed metal spikes, which won't let in air or water. A chalk cross on a wall or chewing gum on a lamppost can show that a message has been left. Nowadays, spies use **electronic** messages, as well as written ones.

*Secret messages, money, or maps might be rolled up and buried in these **dead drop** spikes.*

Message not sent

Some terrorists share e-mail accounts, writing draft messages to each other but never sending them. Governments can't scan unsent e-mails, so they aren't spotted.

rot to break down or decay   **electronic** using or controlled by computers

In 2006, the Russian government said they'd caught British spies who had been using a message transmitter disguised as a rock.

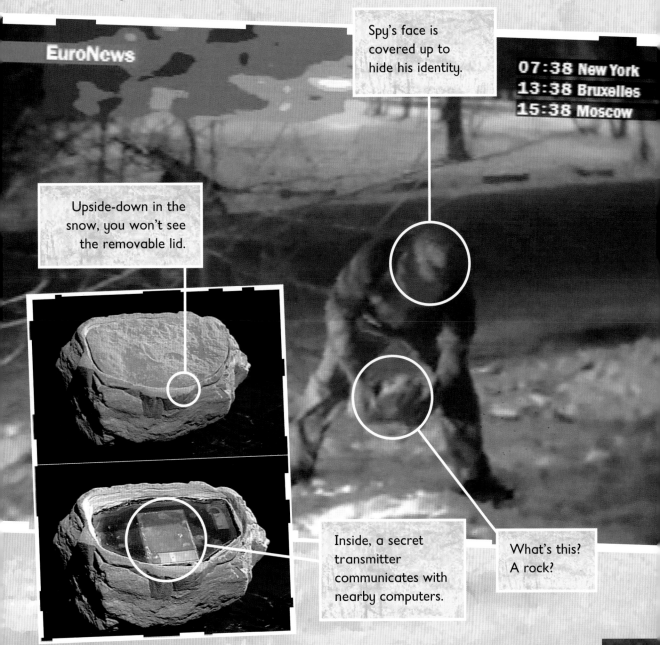

Spy's face is covered up to hide his identity.

EuroNews

07:38 New York
13:38 Bruxelles
15:38 Moscow

Upside-down in the snow, you won't see the removable lid.

Inside, a secret transmitter communicates with nearby computers.

What's this? A rock?

dead drop (or dead-letter box) a place where hidden messages are left

21

Gobbledygook?

Spies need to tell each other things without any of their enemies understanding. That's why they make up brain-boggling, gobbledygook codes.

The science of code making and breaking is called cryptography. When codes were first invented, they had to be cracked by brainy people using pens and paper! Then special machines were invented to do the job. These days spies use **supercomputers** to turn words, numbers, and even pictures into code—and translate them back again.

This code-making, code-breaking machine called Enigma was invented at the end of World War I.

*The third U.S. president, Thomas Jefferson, invented this **cipher** wheel.*

supercomputers very advanced computers that work extremely quickly

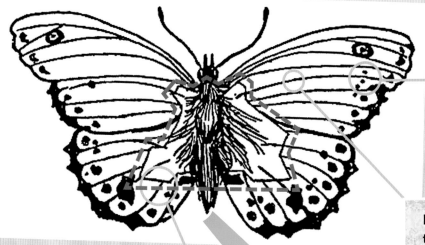

Dots on the wings stand for guns.

Lines lead into the fort, showing where the guns are positioned.

Some spies hid secret maps in drawings. Inside this picture of a butterfly is a map of a fort and its guns.

Outline of fort

A heavy read

The British Navy used to write codes in books with heavy lead covers. If a ship was captured, the crew could throw the books overboard, and they'd quickly sink.

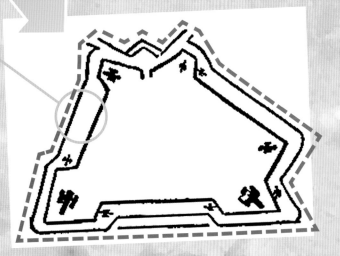

Moving the wing dots inward showed where the guns were kept.

cipher a way of replacing each letter in a message with another letter to hide its meaning

Disappearing words

No matter how good your eyesight, some secret messages are impossible to see. Spies aren't magicians—but they can make their writing disappear!

A **microdot** camera can take a picture so small it would fit this whole page into a period! During World War II, spies sneaked many secret plans past the enemy in this way.

A microdot message was impossible to read—unless you had a microscope. Lenses in the microscope made the dot look hundreds of times bigger, and so the writing became clear.

Lemon juice is used as invisible ink in the film National Treasure. Onion juice, milk, and soapy water work, too!

Invisible ink

If you write a message in lemon juice, no one can see it. But heat it up on a radiator, and the words will magically reappear! Spies use chemical **reactions** like this to create all sorts of invisible inks.

microdot a tiny dot that contains secret information

1 At first glance, this looks like an ordinary watch.

2 Look closer and you can see a tiny smudgy mark at the bottom of the watch face.

SWISS MADE

More than just a gift from one spy to another— this watch carried top-secret information.

3 Under a microscope, all becomes clear—it's a secret message.

Kopfschlus...
...ntwers
1 2 3 4 5...
...onderschüssel
...e r g h i j...
2 2 ... 4 - 5 6 7
...Buchstaben ...ullbuchsta...
...sselungstag. Schieberschl...
...bt den Buchstaben des ...

reaction a chemical change caused by heating or mixing chemicals

Truth and lies

What does a spy dread most? Getting caught! It's hard to hide what you're up to when spy-catchers have machines that can tell if you're fibbing.

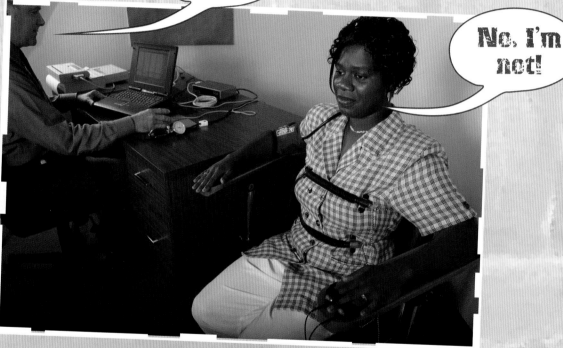

Is she telling the truth? A lie detector (or polygraph) will reveal the answer.

Even if you're a brilliant actor, tiny changes in your body can give you away as an **impostor**. When you're nervous, your heart pumps faster—and this can happen when you're lying, too. Lie detectors measure your **heart rate** as well as how much you sweat, how quickly you are breathing, and other things that show you might be hiding something.

impostor someone pretending to be someone else

26

A voice-recognition system can help to detect an impostor.

Shape of your mouth and throat affects your voice.

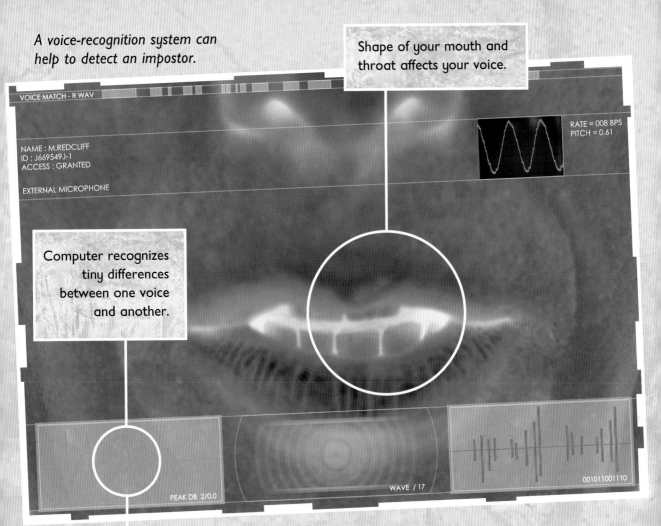

VOICE MATCH - R WAV

RATE = 008 BPS
PITCH = 0.61

NAME : M.REDCLIFF
ID : J669549J-1
ACCESS : GRANTED

EXTERNAL MICROPHONE

Computer recognizes tiny differences between one voice and another.

Even voices that sound the same to a human ear look different on the computer screen.

PEAK DB 2/0.0

WAVE / 17

001011001110

Brain wave

People can train their bodies to cheat lie detectors. But new types of machines that scan the brain may be able to catch even the cleverest spies.

heart rate the number of times your heart beats in one minute

Kiss of death

Spies love secret weapons, from poisoned knitting needles to lipsticks with guns inside. Throughout the years there have been more deadly gadgets than in a James Bond film.

An accident waiting to happen? This exploding plaster cast was used in the Bond film Goldeneye.

No smoking!

Stories say that in the 1960s, U.S. spies planned to kill Cuban leader Fidel Castro—using an exploding cigar! The plot probably didn't really exist, though.

Some famous hidden weapons include a pipe with a pistol inside, a chocolate bar bomb, and an umbrella with a poisoned spike. The more ordinary the object, the bigger the deadly surprise!

In the past, a good hiding place and a bit of imagination allowed spies to get away with murder. But today's **metal detectors**, **X-ray** machines, and sniffer dogs can find even the best secret weapons.

metal detectors devices that use magnets to find hidden metal

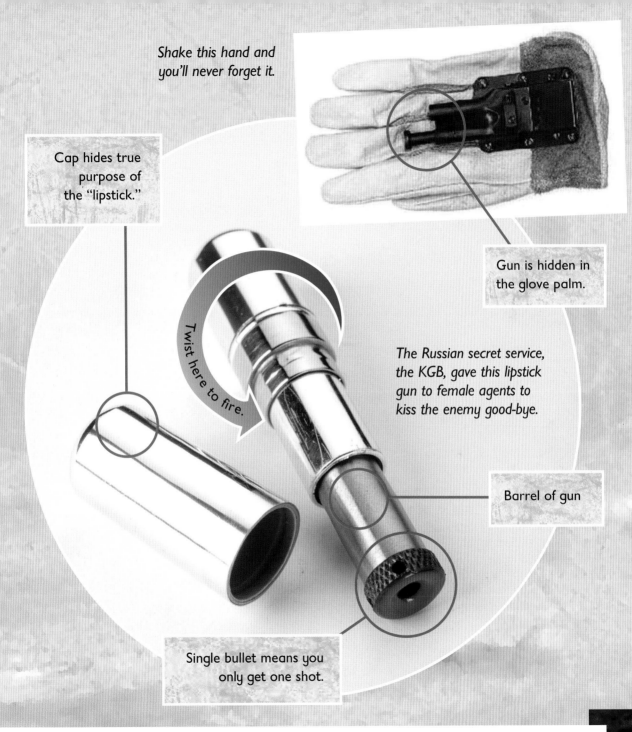

Shake this hand and you'll never forget it.

Cap hides true purpose of the "lipstick."

Gun is hidden in the glove palm.

Twist here to fire.

The Russian secret service, the KGB, gave this lipstick gun to female agents to kiss the enemy good-bye.

Barrel of gun

Single bullet means you only get one shot.

X-rays invisible waves of energy that can be used to see through objects

Glossary

bug a device that records and transmits (sends) sounds to special receivers

CCTV (closed-circuit TV) a way of filming streets, shops, and other places

cipher a way of replacing each letter in a message with another letter to hide its meaning

cover a false identity

dead drop (or dead-letter box) a place where hidden messages are left

electronic using or controlled by computers

gravity a pulling force between all objects in the universe

heart rate the number of times your heart beats in one minute

impostor someone pretending to be someone else

intelligence secret information, especially from governments and armies

intelligence networks groups of spies working for governments or businesses

metal detectors devices that use magnets to find hidden metal

microdot a tiny dot that contains secret information

night vision ability to see in the dark using infrared heat energy

prism a triangular block of glass or plastic that can bend the path of light

radio waves waves of energy that travel silently and invisibly through the air

radome a weatherproof dome covering radio receivers

reaction a chemical change caused by heating or mixing chemicals

reflect to bounce back rays of light

remote control operating a device from a distance, often using radio signals

rot to break down or decay

satellite a machine that is sent into space to collect and send back information

silencer a device that absorbs the sound from a gun, making it much quieter

supercomputers very advanced computers that work extremely quickly

thermal imaging making pictures using infrared heat energy instead of light

voice changer a device that changes the sound of your voice

X-rays invisible waves of energy that can be used to see through objects

Further information

Books

Secrets, Lies, Gizmos, and Spies: A History of Spies and Espionage by Janet Wyman Coleman (Harry N. Abrams, Inc, 2006)
A full history of spying through the ages with lots of excellent photographs from the International Spy Museum in the United States.

Spies by Clive Gifford (Kingfisher Books, 2007)
Plenty of information on codes, disguises, and famous spies through the ages.

web sites

FactHound offers a safe, fun way to find Internet sites related to this book. All of the sites on FactHound have been researched by our staff. Visit *www.facthound.com* for age-appropriate sites. You may browse subjects by clicking on letters, or by clicking on pictures and words.
FactHound will fetch the best sites for you!

Films

Spy Kids directed by Robert Rodriguez (Miramax Films, 2001)
A funny and exciting film about a brother and sister who have to help their spy parents out on missions. Features lots of cool gadgets.

Stormbreaker directed by Geoffrey Sax (Entertainment Film Distributors, 2006)
Almost as great as the book; Alex Rider is a teenager who joins the British secret services. Fun for adults and children with an all-star cast.

National Treasure directed by Jon Turteltaub (Buena Vista Pictures, 2004)
A treasure hunter uses codes and other spy techniques to track down lost treasure.

Index